T0043772

Transportation Then and Now

James Styring

Contents

OXFORD
UNIVERSITY PRESS

OXFORD
UNIVERSITY PRESS

Great Clarendon Street, Oxford OX2 6DP

Oxford University Press is a department of the University of Oxford. It furthers the University's objective of excellence in research, scholarship, and education by publishing worldwide in

Oxford New York

Auckland Cape Town Dar es Salaam Hong Kong Karachi Kuala Lumpur Madrid Melbourne Mexico City Nairobi New Delhi Shanghai Taipei Toronto

With offices in

Argentina Austria Brazil Chile Czech Republic France Greece Guatemala Hungary Italy Japan Poland Portugal Singapore South Korea Switzerland Thailand Turkey Ukraine Vietnam

OXFORD and OXFORD ENGLISH are registered trade marks of Oxford University Press in the UK and in certain other countries

© Oxford University Press 2010

The moral rights of the author have been asserted

Database right Oxford University Press (maker)

First published 2010

2014 2013 2012 2011 2010
10 9 8 7 6 5 4 3 2

No unauthorized photocopying

ISBN: 978 0 19 464499 0

An Audio CD Pack containing this book and a CD is also available
ISBN: 978 0 19 464539 3
The CD has a choice of American and British English recordings of the complete text.

An accompanying Activity Book is also available
ISBN: 978 0 19 464509 6

Printed in China
This book is printed on paper from certified and well-managed sources

ACKNOWLEDGEMENTS

Illustrations by: William Donohoe pp 6 (market), 9 (ships); Rebecca Halls/The Organisation pp 5, 6 (map), 11, 13; Kelly Kennedy pp 19, 23; Ian Moores Graphics pp 22, 26, 44, 46; Dusan Pavlic pp 36, 38, 48.

The Publishers would also like to thank the following for their kind permission to reproduce photographs and other copyright material: Action Plus Sports Images p 18 (Steve Bardens/recumbent bike); Alamy pp 4 (STOCKFOLIO ®), 5 (John White Photos), 10 (Bob Henry), 14 (G P Bowater), 15 (Natrow Images), 20 (The Print Collector), 23 (Motoring Picture Library/Peel P50), 28 (© Bryan & Cherry Alexander Photography), 29 (ISP Photography), 30 (Peter Barritt), 31 (Carsten Leuzinger/ imagebroker/dog), 35 (Simon Holdcroft/jet pack); Corbis pp 23 (Bruce Benedict/TRANSTOCK/Bugatti), 33 (Kimimasa Mayama); Getty Images pp 8 (Keystone/Stringer/Hulton Archive/Kon Tiki), 11 (AFP), 12 (Hulton Archive), 13 (Chung Sung-Jun), 16 (Hulton Archive), 19 (Getty Images), 27 (AFP/ Yves Rossy); Maarten Udema Photography p 8 (canoe); NASA Images pp 27 (Daedalus), 34; Oxford Picture Library p 31 (Chris Andrews/punting); Oxford University Press pp 3, 7, 9, 17, 18 (BMX), 24, 25, 42; PA Photos p 35 (Segway); Skysails GmbH & Co. KG. All rights reserved p 32; TopFoto p 21 (The Granger Collection).

Introduction

Transportation is the movement of people or goods from one place to another. We can transport things in the water, in the air, or over land. We can use animals, vehicles, or just our feet. Sometimes we travel for work, and sometimes for vacation or just for fun.

What transportation can you see here?
What transportation have you used?
What other transportation do you know?

Now read and discover more about transportation!

Then and Now

Until about 7,000 years ago, people had to walk everywhere. Then they started to use animals for transportation. Later, people invented vehicles.

Camels in the Sahara Desert, Africa

Animals

People used horses and donkeys for transportation in lots of places. People also used camels in Africa, elephants in Asia, and llamas in South America. People still use animals for transportation today.

The First Vehicles

People made rafts from tree trunks. They floated on their rafts along rivers and on lakes. It was easier than swimming, and they didn't get wet. These were the first vehicles.

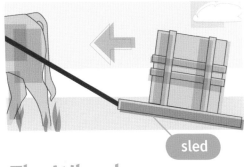

sled

Sleds were like rafts, but they were used on land. They were useful because it's easier to pull heavy things than to lift them.

The Wheel

About 5,500 years ago, people added wheels to sleds. Farmers and traders made carts with two or four wooden wheels. Cows and horses pulled the carts. Carts with wheels were much faster than sleds.

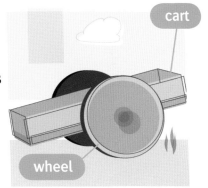

cart

wheel

The wheel is one of the most important inventions in history, and today you can see wheels everywhere. Cars, buses, trucks, trains, bicycles, motorcycles, and planes all have wheels. Wheels are important in engines, too.

A Road Train

trailer

Discover!

A truck with a lot of trailers is called a road train. The longest road train was Australian. It had 117 trailers with 2,126 wheels!

International Transportation

Until about 10,000 years ago, people lived in small family groups and they didn't travel a lot. Then, as villages and towns became bigger, people had to travel to find food. People used animals to carry goods like meat and fur.

Ships Trading in the Middle East

Then about 6,000 years ago, people started to travel long distances to trade metals, salt, and spices. Ships began trading in the Middle East 4,500 years ago. People used ships because animals could not travel over water. Soon, people were trading all around Europe and Asia.

Discover!

Traders took Chinese silk to Europe along the Silk Road 2,500 years ago. They used horses and camels to carry the silk more than 3,000 kilometers.

EUROPE

Silk Road

CHINA

Transportation Today

Today, every country in the world uses water, air, and land transportation to trade food, fuel, clothes, and other goods like cars and televisions.

Tourists started to go on vacation by train and boat 200 years ago. From about 1960, with the invention of large passenger planes, tourism became very popular. Today, about 900 million tourists travel to another country every year.

In 2001, an American called Dennis Tito was the first space tourist. He flew in a Russian spaceship to the International Space Station. Will tourists travel to the moon one day?

→ Go to pages 36–37 for activities.

7

2 Boats and Ships

We use boats and ships to transport passengers and freight. Boats and ships can travel along rivers and across lakes and oceans. What boats or ships have you traveled on?

paddle

A Canoe Called a Kayak

The First Boats

The first vehicles that people used on water were rafts made from tree trunks. Then more than 5,000 years ago, people made canoes. They used paddles to power their canoes. People still use canoes today.

Discover!

In 1947, Thor Heyerdahl built a raft similar to the ancient rafts. He sailed *Kon-Tiki* 8,000 kilometers from Peru to an island in the Pacific Ocean.

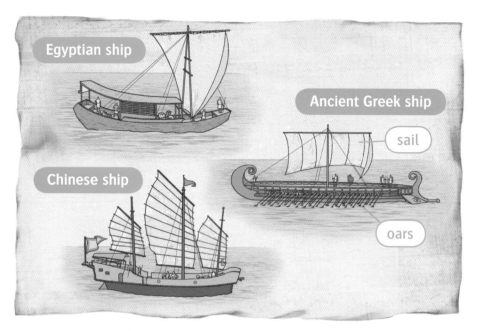

Egyptian ship

Ancient Greek ship

sail

Chinese ship

oars

The First Ships

Egyptian traders sailed the first ships about 4,500 years ago on the River Nile. Later, the Ancient Greeks sailed larger ships around the Mediterranean Sea. Their ships were fast because they used sails, and at the same time men rowed with oars. Traders sailed between the Middle East and India in small ships with triangular sails. Chinese, Korean, and Japanese traders had large ships with square sails.

Chinese people invented the compass about 2,000 years ago. Compasses point to north, and they help people to sail in the right direction across oceans. They are still important for sailors today.

Sailing Around the World

The Vikings lived in Denmark, Norway, and Sweden about 1,000 years ago. They sailed around Europe, and they crossed the Atlantic Ocean to Canada. At the same time, hundreds of ships were trading between Japan, Korea, China, and countries in Southeast Asia.

From about 1500, European ships sailed to North and South America, Africa, and Asia. Their journeys sometimes took years. A lot of ships sank during storms. The ships were small and the sailors were brave. Pirates often attacked ships and stole gold and silver.

After about 1800, ships became important for international trade in goods like coffee, tea, and spices. Ships became bigger, and they had a lot of sails to help them go faster.

An Old Spanish Trading Ship

Ships with Engines

Steam engines powered most ships after about 1850.
Steam ships had propellers and they were faster than
sailing ships. Today, we make modern ships from
metal, and their engines use oil or diesel. There are
about 35,000 commercial ships around the world.
Freighters carry food and clothes, supertankers
transport oil, and cruise ships carry passengers on
vacation. Korea builds the most ships in the world.

Discover!

Some supertankers
are as long as the tallest
skyscrapers. *Knock Nevis*
is 458 meters long.
Sailors use bicycles to
travel along the ship!

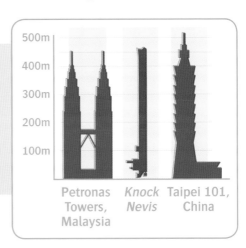

Petronas Towers, Malaysia   *Knock Nevis*   Taipei 101, China

Go to pages 38–39 for activities.

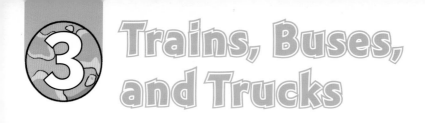

Trains, Buses, and Trucks

Transportation became much faster after the invention of engines. We use buses to transport people and goods, trucks to transport freight, and trains to transport people and freight.

Trains

In 1804, Richard Trevithick built the first train in Wales in the United Kingdom. Its steam engine used coal to heat water. The hot water made steam, and the steam powered the engine. The train moved along two metal tracks called a railroad. In 1825, the world's first railroad system opened in the United Kingdom. Soon, railroads with steam trains were common all around the world. By 1930, steam trains could travel at about 150 kilometers per hour.

An American Steam Train

A Korean High-Speed Train (KTX)

In 1862 the first underground train system opened in London in the United Kingdom. Today, more than 160 cities around the world have underground trains.

Modern trains have electric motors or diesel engines. Some long-distance trains have restaurants, and sleeper cars with beds for passengers to sleep in. Trains are good because they use less fuel per passenger than cars, buses, or planes. Some high-speed trains can travel at more than 300 kilometers per hour.

Discover!

The longest train journey in the world is 9,288 kilometers. The Trans-Siberian Express takes six days to travel across Russia, from Moscow to Vladivostok.

RUSSIA

Moscow

Vladivostok

Buses

Horses pulled the first buses 200 years ago. Buses became popular as cities became bigger, because people traveled on buses to get to work. Modern buses have diesel engines or electric motors. Most buses can carry more than 40 passengers, and some very long, articulated buses can carry 120 people. In many countries, special buses take children to school. In places with no trains, buses carry passengers long distances between cities.

In some countries, buses carry a lot of passengers and goods. Where the hills are very big, people use trucks instead of buses because they are more powerful.

An Indian Bus

Trucks

Trains can only go on railroads, but trucks can go anywhere where there are roads. Trucks can carry many different things. Tanker trucks carry gasoline or milk. Refrigerator trucks keep food cold. In mining areas, people use huge trucks to carry coal and rocks.

Long trucks often have a cab for the driver and a separate trailer for the freight. The cab with a separate trailer helps long trucks to turn. Some cabs have a bed, so the driver can drive a long distance and then stop and sleep.

Discover!

One of the biggest trucks in the world is the Terex Titan in Canada. Each wheel is bigger than two people!

Go to pages 40–41 for activities.

Bicycles and Motorcycles

In busy cities, bicycles and motorcycles are useful. They are narrow, so they can go past cars and buses in traffic jams. Can you ride a bicycle?

Bicycles

The first bicycles were made of wood. Then after 1850 they were made of metal. Early bicycles, called high-wheel bicycles, were uncomfortable because they had no tires. The front wheel was very big, and there were no gears or brakes. Cyclists often crashed.

Modern bicycles are safer because they have brakes and their wheels are both the same size. They also have rubber tires so they are comfortable. People cycle to work or school, and for fun and sport. Bicycles are good because they don't produce pollution.

A High-Wheel Bicycle

Discover!

There are 1,000 million bicycles in the world, and only 600 million cars.

How Bicycles Work

The cyclist sits on the saddle and turns the pedals. The pedals move the chain, and the chain powers the back wheel. Gears help the bicycle to go faster, or to go up hills. The cyclist stops the bicycle with the brakes. It's good for cyclists to wear a helmet and gloves. These protect their head and hands in a fall or a crash.

The Parts of a Bicycle

helmet

glove

brake

frame

saddle

tire

gears

pedal

chain

front wheel

back wheel

Types of Bicycle

BMX bicycles are small. They are for doing tricks. Mountain bikes are for off-road cycling, so they have thick tires and strong frames. Mountain bikes are one of the most popular types of bicycle.

Racing bikes are light. They have narrow tires, and they can travel at 40 kilometers per hour. The most famous bicycle race is the *Tour de France* in Europe. The race is about 3,500 kilometers and it usually takes 23 days every summer.

A BMX Rider Doing a Trick

Recumbent bicycles look funny, but they are very comfortable. The cyclist lies down and the pedals are at the front of the bicycle.

Riding a Recumbent Bicycle

Discover!

In 2008, Mark Beaumont cycled 29,440 kilometers around the world. He visited 20 countries in 194 days.

Motorcycles

Motorcycles can carry one or two people. The engine powers the back wheel with a chain, like a bicycle. Motorcycles are heavier than bicycles, and they have a strong, metal frame, and thick tires. Motorcyclists have to wear a helmet and leather clothes to protect themselves. Motorcycle racing is a popular sport. The riders lean very near to the ground so that they can turn quickly. Some motorcycles can go faster than 300 kilometers per hour!

Discover!

In 1991, Yasuyuki Kudo rode for 331 kilometers on the back wheel of his motorcycle in Tsukuba, Japan.

Go to pages 42–43 for activities.

Cars are the most popular type of motorized transportation. We use cars to go to work or school, to go shopping, and for vacation. There are family cars, fast sports cars, and special cars like police cars and taxis.

The History of Cars

Can you imagine a world without cars? We have only had cars for about 120 years. People laughed at the first cars. They were slow and noisy. Two German engineers, Daimler and Benz, made the first car with a gasoline engine in 1885. It only had three wheels.

A Daimler-Benz Three-Wheeled Car

From about 1905, companies like Rolls-Royce started to make cars. They were very expensive because people made each car by hand. Then, in 1913, the Ford Motor Company started to make their Model T car in a special factory. Ford's factories produced cars quickly, so the Model T was less expensive than other cars. By 1927, there were more than 15 million Model Ts on the roads.

Gasoline in the USA was cheap and people wanted to travel long distances, so by 1950, American cars were large. In Europe and Asia, drivers preferred small cars that were better in city traffic.

How Cars Work

Most cars have a gasoline or a diesel engine. The driver starts the engine with a key. The engine can power the front wheels, the back wheels, or all four wheels. The driver uses the pedals to go faster, to change gears, and to stop. Drivers of automatic cars don't need to change the gears. Cars usually have five gears for going forward and one gear for going backward. The driver turns the steering wheel and the steering wheel turns the front wheels. You have to wear a seat belt to protect yourself if there is a crash. Airbags also protect you, but older cars don't have them.

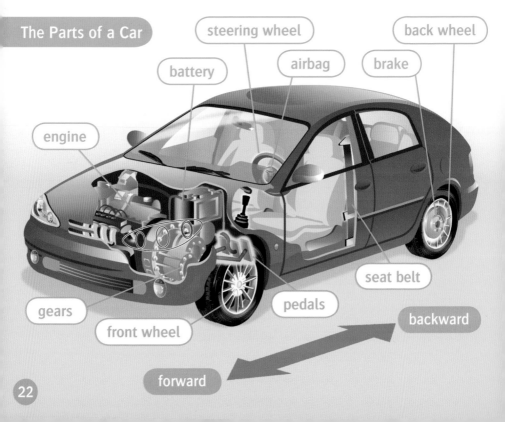

The Parts of a Car

steering wheel

back wheel

battery

airbag

brake

engine

seat belt

gears

pedals

backward

front wheel

forward

Cool Cars

Sports cars, like the Bugatti Veyron, are low. This helps the car to go fast because air can move easily over it. The

A Bugatti Veyron

Bugatti Veyron goes faster than 400 kilometers per hour. It costs 1.5 million US dollars, and the people who make the cars have only sold a few hundred since they started to produce them in 2005.

A Peel P50

The Peel P50 is the smallest car in the world. It was first made in 1963. It's 134 centimeters long and 99 centimeters wide. Its top speed is 61 kilometers per hour.

Discover!

The world's longest car is the American Dream. It has 24 wheels and it's 30.5 meters long! It has a swimming pool, and a helicopter can land on it.

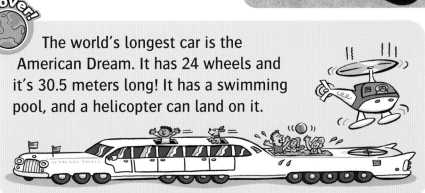

Go to pages 44–45 for activities.

6 Aircraft

People have dreamed about flying for thousands of years, but there weren't any planes until just over 100 years ago. Before planes, people flew in hot-air balloons.

Hot-Air Balloons

How do hot-air balloons fly? Hot air goes up. A fire under the balloon heats the air inside the balloon, so the balloon goes up. In France in 1793, the Montgolfier brothers built the first hot-air balloon for passengers.

Airships

Airships were popular between 1900 and 1940, and they are popular again now. Inside an airship, there's a gas that is lighter than air. This makes the airship stay in the air. Airships have engines and they can fly at 90 kilometers per hour.

A Modern Airship

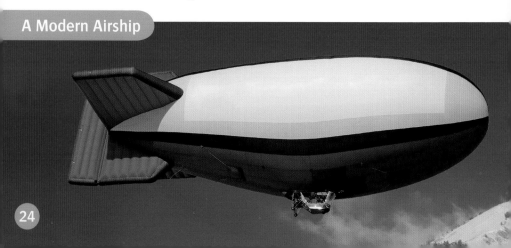

Concorde

Planes

Planes have changed a lot since the first flight by the Wright brothers in 1903. For many years, planes were wooden, and they had two pairs of wings.

Today, people make planes from very thin metal and plastics. Airliners can carry hundreds of passengers and their bags. Planes carry freight and letters, too. Some very rich people have their own small plane.

Concorde was an airliner that flew between 1976 and 2003. It could fly from Europe to the USA in three hours and 20 minutes – twice as fast as other airliners. It flew at 2,140 kilometers per hour.

Discover! The biggest airliner is the Airbus A380. It can carry more than 850 passengers. It's a double-decker and its wings are longer than a soccer pitch!

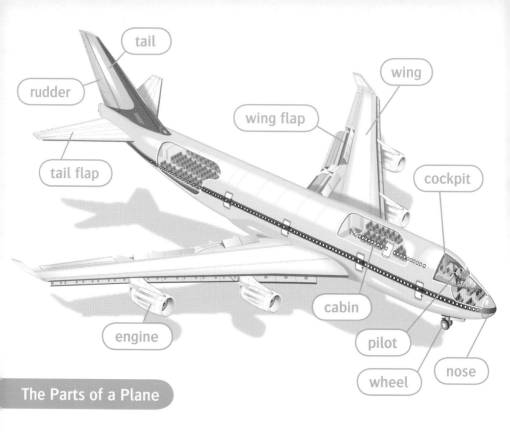

tail

rudder

wing

wing flap

tail flap

cockpit

cabin

engine

pilot

nose

wheel

The Parts of a Plane

How Planes Work

Planes usually have engines on the wings. The wings are a special shape. When air goes over the wings fast, the air under the wings pushes the plane up, and it flies. The engines make the plane go very fast.

Pilots sit in the cockpit, at the front of the plane. They use the rudder to turn left and right, and they use the tail flaps to go up and down. The wing flaps control the speed. Passengers sit in the cabin.

Other Types of Aircraft

The Daedalus is a very light plane. A person pedals the plane, like a bicycle.

Helicopters have rotors above the cabin. The rotors lift the helicopter into the air. Helicopters are useful because they can keep still in the air and they can fly in any direction. Planes can only go forward.

Planes with skis instead of wheels can land on snow. There are also special seaplanes that can land on water. Space shuttles and rockets take astronauts and machines into space.

Discover!

Yves Rossy, from France, is called Rocket Man. He has built a very small plane with four engines on the wings.

Go to pages 46–47 for activities.

27

Around the World

Most places in the world have vehicles like cars and bicycles, but some places have special types of transportation. What do you think these are?

Transportation in Nunavut

snowmobile

dog sled

Nunavut, Canada

It's very cold in Nunavut in the north of Canada. Some Inuit people use dogs to pull their sleds over the ice and snow. Today, many people also travel by snowmobile – a small, motorized vehicle.

Khangai, Mongolia

In Mongolia, roads and railroads go between cities, but in the Khangai mountains there aren't many vehicles. Farmer use a donkey or an ox to pull their carts. Traders use camel to transport goods over mountains and across deserts. People also travel long distances on horses.

Boats in Venice

water bus

water taxi

gondola

Venice, Italy

There aren't any cars, buses, trucks, or even bicycles in Venice. This is because there are no roads. The city was built on a lot of small islands and there are bridges between them. People walk on small roads called paths, and over bridges, but most journeys in Venice are by boat.

People take water buses to work and to school, and water taxis to the airport and to the train station. Ambulances and fire engines are boats, too! The people of Venice have traveled by gondola for hundreds of years. A gondolier stands at the back and powers the gondola with an oar. Today, most gondolas are for the tourists.

Delhi, India

Delhi is a busy city, and the traffic is slow.
Most people travel on buses, trains, or
underground trains.

Bicycles and rickshaws are also popular.
A rickshaw is a cart for goods or passengers.
A rickshaw has two wheels and a person pulls
it. A cycle rickshaw has three wheels. The
front is like a bicycle and the driver pedals the
rickshaw. An auto rickshaw has a small engine.
It's the fastest type of rickshaw, but it's noisy
and it makes a lot of pollution.

Rickshaws in Delhi

auto rickshaw

cycle
rickshaw

Oxford, United Kingdom

Oxford is a small city and there aren't many hills, so bicycles are popular. Also, bicycles are cheap and people enjoy cycling in the fresh air. Many of the city's streets are small and old, so it's much quicker to travel by bicycle than by car or bus. Some cyclists carry their shopping and even their dogs in baskets or bicycle trailers.

People enjoy punting on the river in Oxford. A punt is a wooden river boat. To move the punt, you push on the bottom of the river with a long wooden or metal pole.

Punting in Oxford

pole

punt

Go to pages 48–49 for activities.

8 In the Future

The world needs to produce less pollution. Electric motors produce less pollution than diesel and gasoline engines. Will all vehicles have electric motors one day? What will transportation be like in the future?

Cars

Some modern cars use biodiesel. Biodiesel comes from plants, and it's a clean fuel. We can also produce clean energy from the sun and the wind. Machines can put this energy into batteries that power electric motors. In the future, most cars will have electric motors or they will use biodiesel.

A Ship with A Modern Sail

Copyright SkySails

Ships

After 100 years of ships with engines, sails will be important again for ships in the future. Sails will help to power ships, so they use less fuel.

The Dream Cup Solar Car Race, Japan

Solar Vehicles

In some countries where it's very sunny, there are solar cars. They use energy from the sun. Most solar cars are racing cars. The fastest solar cars travel up to 90 kilometers per hour.

People have made some solar planes, too. Solar planes are very light and they can't carry much. Maybe more vehicles in the future will use solar energy.

Trains

Maglev trains use magnets to float in the air above the track. They are much faster than usual trains. Will maglev trains be common in the future?

Air Travel

Passenger planes with scramjet engines will fly faster than 5,000 kilometers per hour. A scramjet plane will fly from New York in the USA to Hong Kong in China in 90 minutes. This journey takes 14 hours in an airliner. The only problem with going fast is that it uses a lot of fuel, which produces more pollution.

A Design for a Space Plane

Space Travel

Do you dream of being an astronaut? Perhaps your dream will come true! Soon, tourists will be able to travel a long way above Earth in space planes. Space tourists will see Earth from space. It won't be cheap, but it will be an amazing experience.

What Next?

What transportation will you use in the future? What about an electric bicycle? It has a small electric motor that makes it easier to pedal quickly. An electric bicycle is great for going up hills.

Or do you want to try a personal transporter? It has two wheels and an electric motor. You lean forward to go forward, and to the left or the right to turn. It can travel at 20 kilometers per hour.

A Personal Transporter

A Jet Pack

A jet pack has one or two jet engines, but it doesn't have any wings. It can fly anywhere! Do you want to try a jet pack? Where will you fly?

→ Go to pages 50–51 for activities.

① Then and Now

← Read pages 4–7.

1 **Write the words.**

camel   ~~cart~~   ship   sled   spaceship   trailer

1 ___cart___

2 _____

3 _____

4 _____

5 _____

6 _____

2 **Does it have wheels? Write *yes* or *no*.**

1 a sled   ___no___

2 a motorcycle   _____

3 a raft   _____

4 a car   _____

5 a cart   _____

6 an engine   _____

3 Find the words. Then complete the chart.

bicycle camel bus boat donkey salt elephant fuel horse llama food silk train spice struck

Animals	Vehicles	Goods
_____	_bicycle_	_____
_____	_____	_____
_____	_____	_____
_____	_____	_____
_____	_____	_____

4 Answer the questions.

1 How did people travel before there were vehicles?

   People walked or they used animals.

2 Why were sleds useful?

   _____

3 What was one of the most important inventions in history?

   _____

4 Why did people start to travel 10,000 years ago?

   _____

5 How long is the Silk Road?

   _____

6 How did Dennis Tito travel to the International Space Station?

   _____

2 Boats and Ships

← Read pages 8–11.

1 Write the words.

| paddle | compass | oar | propeller | sail | steam engine |

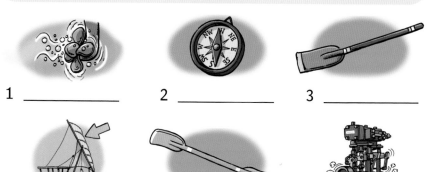

1 _____ 2 _____ 3 _____

4 _____ 5 _____ 6 _____

2 Write true or false.

1 The first canoes were made from tree trunks. _true_

2 People powered canoes with steam engines. _____

3 Chinese ships had triangular sails. _____

4 The Ancient Greeks sailed to Canada. _____

5 Pirates stole gold and silver. _____

6 A cruise ship is a passenger ship. _____

3 Number the vehicles in order. 1 = earliest, 5 = latest.

☐ canoes   ☐ supertankers

☐ steam ships   ☐ sailing ships   1 rafts

4 Match.

1 Thor Heyerdahl sailed from Peru

2 Egyptian sailors sailed on

3 The Ancient Greeks sailed around

4 The Vikings lived in

5 The Vikings sailed across

6 Traders sailed between Japan, Korea, China,

the Atlantic Ocean.

the Mediterranean Sea.

Denmark, Sweden, and Norway.

the River Nile.

and Southeast Asia.

to an island in the Pacific Ocean.

5 Answer the questions.

1 Why were the Ancient Greek ships fast?

_____

2 How do sailors know which direction to sail in?

_____

3 What problems did European sailors have about 500 years ago?

_____

4 What fuels do modern ships use?

_____

5 What ships do tourists use when they go on vacation?

_____

6 How do sailors travel along *Knock Nevis*?

_____

(3) Trains, Buses, and Trucks

← Read pages 12–15.

1 Write the words.

> tanker truck   refrigerator truck   bus
> high-speed train   steam train   articulated bus

1 It's the fastest type of train. _____

2 Its engine uses coal and water. _____

3 It's very long and it carries people on roads. _____

4 It carries gasoline or milk. _____

5 It carries children to school. _____

6 It keeps food cold. _____

2 Write the numbers.

> ~~150~~   160   200   300   9,288

1 By 1930, steam trains could travel at _150_ kilometers per hour.

2 Modern high-speed trains can travel at _____ kilometers per hour.

3 The longest train journey is _____ kilometers.

4 There are underground trains in more than _____ cities around the world.

5 Horses pulled the first buses _____ years ago.

3 Number the vehicles in order. 1 = earliest, 4 = latest.

☐ diesel trains ☐ high-speed trains

☐ underground trains ☐ steam trains

4 Complete the sentences.

coal   steam   coal   engine   steam   water   engine   water

1 Steam engines use _coal_ .

2 The _____ heats _____ .

3 The hot _____ makes _____ .

4 The _____ powers the _____ .

5 The _____ moves the train along the tracks.

5 Answer the questions.

1 Where did people build the first train?

_____

2 What uses the most fuel per passenger, a train or a car?

_____

3 How long does it take the Trans-Siberian Express to travel across Russia?

_____

4 Where was the world's first underground train system?

_____

5 Why did buses become popular?

_____

(4) Bicycles and Motorcyles

← Read pages 16–19.

1 Write the words.

> back wheel   brake   chain   frame
> front wheel   gears   helmet   pedal
> glove   saddle   tire

1 _____

2 _____

3 _____

4 _____

5 _____

6 _____

7 _____

8 _____

9 _____

10 _____

11 _____

2 Complete the sentences.

> comfortable   light   popular   small   strong   thick

1 Racing bikes are _____ .

2 BMX bicycles are _____ .

3 Recumbent bicycles are _____ .

4 Mountain bikes are the most _____ type of bicycle.

5 Their tires are _____ and their frames are _____ .

3 Circle the correct words.

1 Bicycles have **gears** / **an engine**.

2 The *Tour de France* is a famous **motorcycle** / **bicycle race**.

3 The first bicycles were made of **metal** / **wood**.

4 Motorcycles are **slower** / **faster** than bicycles.

4 Write *true* or *false*.

1 Motorcycles and bicycles have chains. _____

2 It's good for cyclists to wear a helmet. _____

3 There are more bicycles in the world than cars. _____

4 Mountain bikes and motorcycles have strong frames. _____

5 Mark Beaumont cycled 29,440 kilometers on his back wheel. _____

6 Bicycles are heavier than motorcycles. _____

5 Answer the questions.

1 Why were the first bicycles uncomfortable?

_____

2 Why do people cycle?

_____

3 How does a cyclist stop the bicycle?

_____

4 Why do racing motorcyclists lean near to the ground?

_____

5 Cars

← Read pages 20–23.

1 Write the words.

brake   engine   front wheel
gears   pedals   back wheel
seat belt   steering wheel

1 _____

2 _____

3 _____

4 _____

5 _____

6 _____

7 _____

8 _____

2 Write *true* or *false*.

1 The first car had four wheels. _____

2 The Ford Model T was expensive to produce. _____

3 Rolls-Royce sold 15 million cars between 1913 and 1927. _____

4 Small cars are good in city traffic. _____

5 Cars usually have six gears. _____

6 A car's steering wheel turns the front wheels. _____

7 Old cars have the biggest airbags. _____

8 The Bugatti Veyron is 134 centimeters long. _____

3 Complete the chart.

were driving large cars.   Ford opened   ~~the first car~~.
15 million Model Ts were   Rolls-Royce
The Peel P50   cars.   was first made.

1885	Daimler and Benz made _the first car_ .
1905	_____ started to make _____ .
1913	_____ the model T factory.
1927	_____ on the road.
1950	Americans _____ .
1963	_____ was first made.
2005	The Bugatti Veyron _____ .

4 Answer the questions.

1 What was the first car like?

_____

2 Why did Americans buy large cars?

_____

3 What does a driver need to start a car?

_____

4 What two things protect the driver and passengers?

_____

5 Why are sports cars low?

_____

6 Aircraft

← Read pages 24–27.

1 Complete the words.

1 t_a_ _i_l

2 r__dd__r

3 w__ng

4 __ng__n__

5 fl__p

6 c__b__n

7 wh__ __l

8 n__s__

9 c__ckp__t

10 p__l__t

2 Match.

1	Concorde stopped flying	1793
2	an airship's speed (kilometers per hour)	90
3	Concorde's speed (kilometers per hour)	1903
4	the first hot-air balloon for passengers	2003
5	the first plane flew	850
6	the passengers that an Airbus A380 can carry	2,140

3 Find and write the aircraft.

s	p	a	c	e	s	h	u	t	t	l	e	d
h	f	b	a	l	l	o	o	n	e	s	r	d
m	g	h	i	d	u	l	e	w	r	s	o	a
p	a	i	r	l	i	n	e	r	t	o	c	i
l	e	r	s	p	e	c	s	h	e	p	k	n
a	t	r	h	e	l	i	c	o	p	t	e	r
n	e	r	i	a	s	t	r	d	e	r	t	s
e	t	r	p	e	n	a	s	t	r	e	r	e

1 _airliner_

2 b_____

3 r_____

4 a_____

5 h_____

6 p_____

7 s_____

_____

4 Answer the questions.

1 Why do balloons go up?

_____

2 What is inside airships?

_____

3 How do planes stay in the air?

_____

4 Where do passengers sit?

_____

5 What powers the Daedalus?

_____

6 Why are helicopters useful?

_____

7 What aircraft have you traveled in?

_____

7 Around the World

← Read pages 28–31.

1 Write the words.

snowmobile   gondola   punt
cycle rickshaw   sled   auto rickshaw

1 _____

2 _____

3 _____

4 _____

5 _____

6 _____

2 Complete the sentences.

cycle rickshaw   gondolier   ox   sled

1 A _____ travels quickly over snow and ice.

2 A Mongolian farmer can use an _____ to pull his cart.

3 A _____ has three wheels, but no engine.

4 A _____ works in Venice.

3 Write the countries. Then write the types of transportation.

> Canada   United Kingdom   India   Italy   Mongolia

1 Khangai   _____   _____

2 Delhi   _____   _____

3 Oxford   _____   _____

4 Nunavut   _____   _____

5 Venice   _____   _____

4 Answer the questions.

1 In Nunavut, how do people travel?

_____

2 What animals do people in Mongolia use for transportation?

_____

3 Why are there no trucks in Venice?

_____

4 What is a gondola?

_____

5 What is the difference between a rickshaw and a cycle rickshaw?

_____

6 How do some people in Oxford transport shopping or dogs?

_____

8 In the Future

← Read pages 32–35.

1 Complete the puzzle.

1 Biodiesel is made from them.

2 It uses energy from the sun.

3 It's a special high-speed engine.

4 It has two wheels, but it isn't a bicycle.

5 It has jet engines, but no wings.

6 They will help to power modern ships.

7 It uses magnets to float above the track.

8 You can travel a long way above Earth in this.

1
p
l
a
n
t
s

2 Does it fly? Write *yes* or *no*.

1 maglev train _____

2 electric car _____

3 solar plane _____

4 scramjet plane _____

5 electric bike _____

6 jet pack _____

3 **Write _true_ or _false_.**

1 Diesel engines produce more pollution than
  electric motors. _____

2 Biodiesel is a clean fuel. _____

3 We can put gasoline into batteries. _____

4 Scramjet planes will use less fuel than
  today's airliners. _____

5 Solar cars are faster than personal
  transporters. _____

4 **Answer the questions.**

1 How will ships use less fuel?

  _____

2 What do we use to make biodiesel?

  _____

3 Where can we get clean energy from?

  _____

4 Why are electric bicycles good for going up hills?

  _____

5 What transportation do you use now? What will you use in
  the future?

  _____

  _____

  _____

  _____

A Transportation Poster

1 Find or draw pictures of two vehicles.

2 Write notes about the vehicles.

Vehicle:

Type of transportation:

What's it made of?

Where does it come from?

Who invented it? When?

Vehicle:

Type of transportation:

What's it made of?

Where does it come from?

Who invented it? When?

3 Write about the vehicles and make a poster.
Display your poster.

A Transportation Survey

1 Write the names of five friends or people from your family at the top of the survey.

2 Ask questions and complete your survey with ✓ or ✗.

Have you traveled in a plane?

Yes, I have!

Have you traveled on a camel?

No, I haven't.

Names					
plane					
helicopter					
sled					
camel					
rickshaw					
bicycle					
motorcycle					
truck					
bus					
canoe					

3 Write about the results. Display your results.

Glossary

aircraft (*plural* **aircraft**) a vehicle that can fly

ambulance a vehicle that takes very sick people to hospital

ancient from thousands of years in the past

area part of a place

attack to fight with someone or something

become to change into; to start to be

bottom the opposite of top

brave not scared

cab where a truck driver sits

canoe a small boat powered with a paddle

carry to take something to another place

change to become different; to make something different

cheap not expensive

child (*plural* **children**) a very young person

coal old wood that you burn to make fire

comfortable nice to be in, for example, soft beds or chairs

commercial about buying and selling

common usual; seen in many places

company a group of people that makes money by producing or selling things

cross to move from one side to another

diesel a type of gasoline; a liquid that burns and powers an engine

direction the position someone or something moves toward

distance the space between two places, for example, meters, kilometers

donkey an animal like a small horse

double-decker a vehicle with two floors

electric using electricity (a type of energy)

energy we need energy to move and grow; machines need energy to work

engine a machine that produces energy to move a vehicle

famous known by many people

ferry a ship that transports people and goods

float to move slowly on water or in the air

freight goods that ships, planes, and trains transport

freighter (*or* **cargo ship**) a ship that carries freight

fresh clean and cool (for air)

fuel something that we use to produce heat or energy

funny unusual or amusing

gas not a solid or liquid; like air

gasoline (*or* **petrol**) a liquid that burns and powers an engine

gold an expensive yellow metal

goods things that we buy and sell

ground the land that we stand on

heat to make something hot

huge very big

imagine to think of a possible situation

invent to make or design something new

invention a new idea or thing

island land with water around it

lake a big area of water

land to fly a plane from the air onto the land

leather the skin of an animal; we use it to make shoes and jackets

lie down to rest in a comfortable place, for example, when we sleep

low not high

metal something hard and made from minerals

mining finding minerals under the ground

modern not from the past

motor an engine, often small or electric

motorized with a motor

move to go from one place to another

narrow thin

noisy making a loud sound

oil a fuel; it's a black liquid used to make gasoline

ox (*plural* **oxen**) an animal like a cow

pair two things the same

passenger someone traveling in, for example, a bus, train, plane, or ship

pedal to push with your feet on a pedal

pirate someone on a ship who attacks and steals things from other ships

plastic a man-made material

pollution something that makes air, land, or water dirty

popular liked by many people

power to make something move or work

powerful having great power; being strong

prefer to like better

problem something that is not easy

produce to grow or make something

propeller a machine that turns quickly to power a ship or aircraft

protect to keep safe from danger

push to make something move away; the opposite of pull

river water on land that goes to the ocean

road vehicles travel on it

rock a very hard natural material

rotor blades, like a propeller, on a helicopter

row to move a boat through water with oars

rubber a soft material that you use to make tires

safe not in danger

sail to travel in a ship or a boat using sails or an engine

sailor someone who works on a ship or a boat

separate not connected; apart

shape for example, circle, square, triangle

ship a large boat

silver an expensive gray metal

similar like someone or something

sink to fall to the bottom of water

size how big or small someone or something is

sleeper car where you can sleep on a train in a bed

soccer pitch (*or* **football pitch**) the place where you play soccer

solar from the sun; using energy from the sun

space where the moon and stars are

spaceship a vehicle that takes astronauts into space

space shuttle a vehicle that takes astronauts into space

space station a building in space where astronauts live and work

special different and important

spice we use it to give flavor to food; it comes from plants

steam the hot gas that water makes when it boils

storm bad weather; lots of wind and rain

street vehicles travel on it

thick not thin

tire (*or* **tyre**) the thick, soft ring on a wheel, made from rubber

top speed the fastest that someone or something can go

town a place with a lot of buildings, larger than a village and smaller than a city

trade to buy and sell things

traffic vehicles moving along a street

traffic jam vehicles that can't move because there are too many other vehicles

transport to take something or someone from one place to another in a vehicle

tree trunk the thick part of a tree

triangular in the shape of a triangle

uncomfortable not comfortable

useful that helps someone to do something

vehicle something for transporting goods or people

village a few houses in the countryside; smaller than a town

without not having something; not doing something

wooden made of wood

Oxford Read and Discover

Series Editor: Hazel Geatches • CLIL Adviser: John Clegg

Oxford Read and Discover graded readers are at four levels, from 3 to 6, suitable for students from age 8 and older. They cover many topics within three subject areas, and can support English across the curriculum, or Content and Language Integrated Learning (CLIL).

Available for each reader:
• Audio CD Pack (book & audio CD)
• Activity Book

For Teacher's Notes & CLIL Guidance go to
www.oup.com/elt/teacher/readanddiscover

Subject Area / Level	The World of Science & Technology	The Natural World	The World of Arts & Social Studies
3 600 headwords	• How We Make Products • Sound and Music • Super Structures • Your Five Senses	• Amazing Minibeasts • Animals in the Air • Life in Rainforests • Wonderful Water	• Festivals Around the World • Free Time Around the World
4 750 headwords	• All About Plants • How to Stay Healthy • Machines Then and Now • Why We Recycle	• All About Desert Life • All About Ocean Life • Animals at Night • Incredible Earth	• Animals in Art • Wonders of the Past
5 900 headwords	• Materials to Products • Medicine Then and Now • Transportation Then and Now • Wild Weather	• All About Islands • Animal Life Cycles • Exploring Our World • Great Migrations	• Homes Around the World • Our World in Art
6 1,050 headwords	• Cells and Microbes • Clothes Then and Now • Incredible Energy • Your Amazing Body	• All About Space • Caring for Our Planet • Earth Then and Now • Wonderful Ecosystems	• Helping Around the World • Food Around the World

For younger students, **Dolphin Readers** Levels Starter, 1, and 2 are available.